Oceans of the World

The Pacific Ocean

By Lauren Gordon

Table of Contents

The Pacific Ocean 3
Words to Know 22
Index 23
Comprehension Questions 23
About the Author 24

A Starfish Book
SEAHORSE PUBLISHING

Teaching Tips for Caregivers:

As a caregiver, you can help your child succeed in school by giving them a strong foundation in language and literacy skills and a desire to learn to read.

This book helps children grow by letting them practice reading skills.

Reading for pleasure and interest will help your child to develop reading skills and will give your child the opportunity to practice these skills in meaningful ways.

- Encourage your child to read on her own at home
- Encourage your child to practice reading aloud
- Encourage activities that require reading
- Establish a reading time
- Talk with your child
- Give your child writing materials

Teaching Tips for Teachers:

Research shows that one of the best ways for students to learn a new topic is to read about it.

Before Reading

- Read the "Words to Know" and discuss the meaning of each word.
- Read the back cover to see what the book is about.

During Reading

- When a student gets to a word that is unknown, ask them to look at the rest of the sentence to find clues to help with the meaning of the unknown word.
- Ask the student to write down any pages of the book that were confusing to them.

After Reading

- Discuss the main idea of the book.
- Ask students to give one detail that they learned in the book by showing a text dependent answer from the book.

The Pacific Ocean

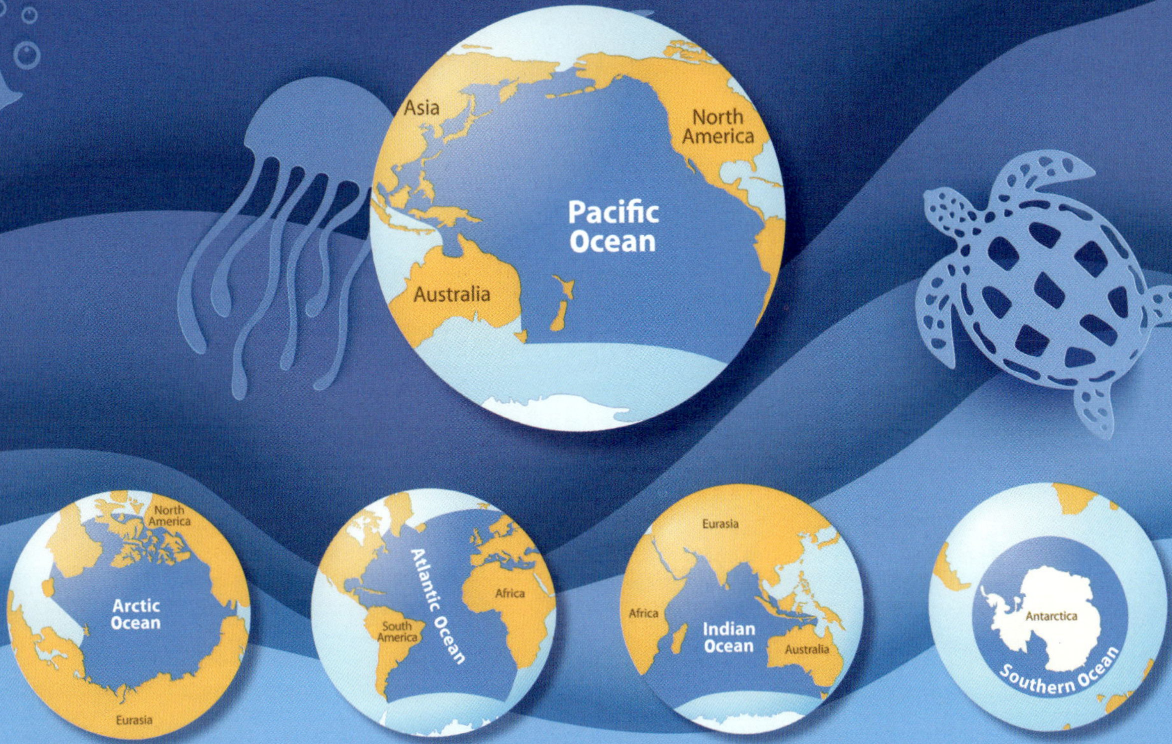

There are five oceans on Earth.
One is the Pacific Ocean.

The Pacific Ocean is vast.

It stretches between the **continents** of North America, South America, Asia, and Australia.

The Pacific Ocean is the largest ocean in the world!

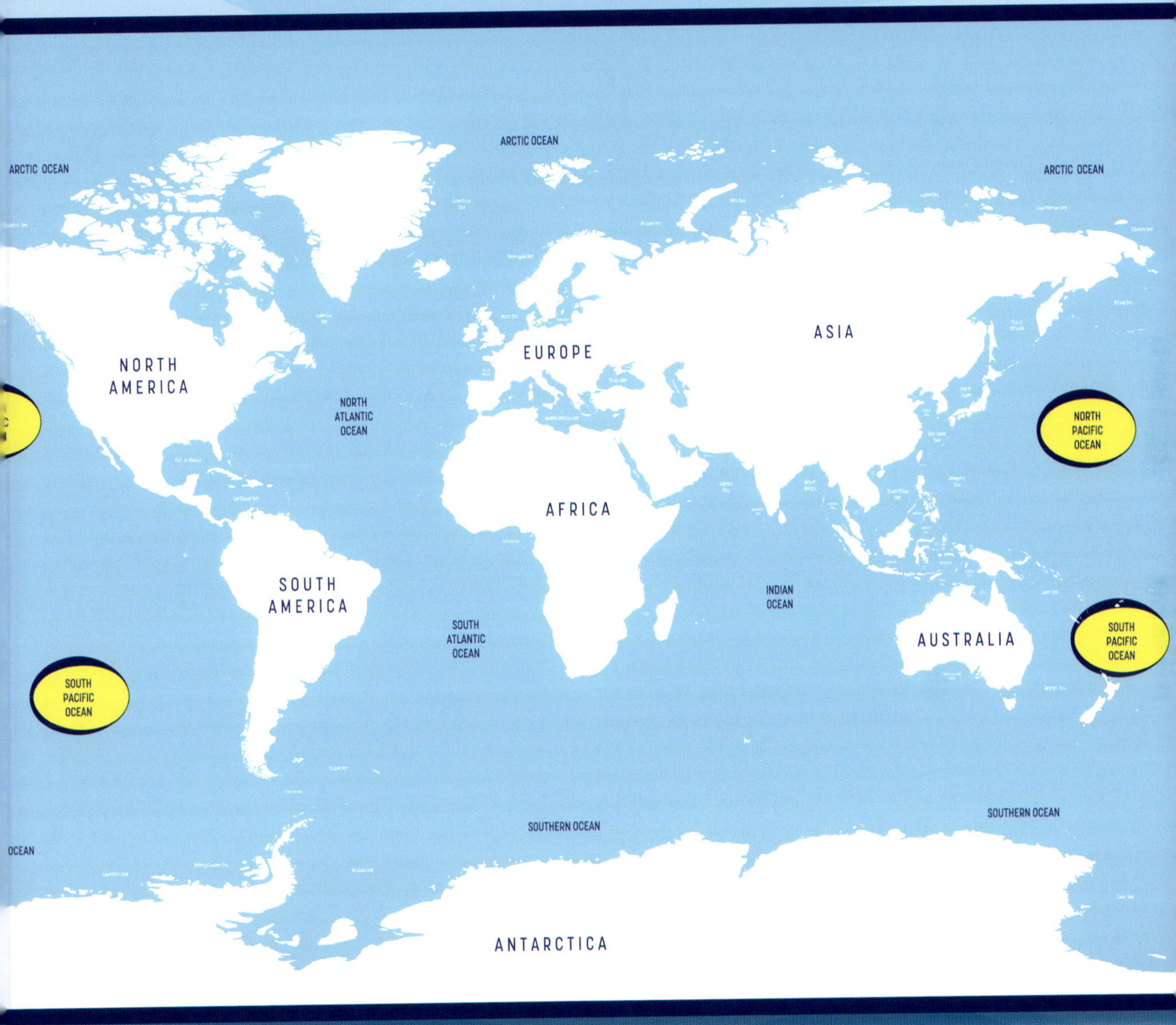
ARCTIC OCEAN
ARCTIC OCEAN
ARCTIC OCEAN
NORTH AMERICA
EUROPE
ASIA
NORTH ATLANTIC OCEAN
NORTH PACIFIC OCEAN
AFRICA
SOUTH AMERICA
INDIAN OCEAN
SOUTH ATLANTIC OCEAN
AUSTRALIA
SOUTH PACIFIC OCEAN
SOUTH PACIFIC OCEAN
SOUTHERN OCEAN
SOUTHERN OCEAN
OCEAN
ANTARCTICA

The **equator** is an imaginary line around the middle of Earth.

It separates the Pacific Ocean into the North Pacific Ocean and the South Pacific Ocean.

Pacific waters are warmer below the equator and cooler above it.

The word *Pacific* means "peaceful."

The Portuguese **explorer** Ferdinand Magellan named the Pacific Ocean in 1521.

Ferdinand Magellan

One of Ferdinand Magellan's ships was the first to sail around the world.

The Pacific Ocean covers about one-third of Earth's surface.

It contains more than half of all the water on the planet.

The Pacific Ocean is bigger than all the continents put together.

The Pacific Ocean is very deep.

It can be up to 35,000 feet (10,670 meters) deep.

That is over six miles (ten kilometers) deep!

The deepest part of the Pacific, and the lowest place on Earth, is in the Mariana Trench.

Most of Earth's volcanoes are in or near the Pacific Ocean.

The volcanoes sometimes cause **earthquakes**.

The Pacific Ocean is home to many animals.

Most of the world's supply of fish is caught in the Pacific.

Big and small mammals live in the Pacific Ocean.

Humpback whales swim in deep waters.

Sea otters float on their backs near the surface.

Sea otters are **endangered** because of pollution, hunting, and disease.

The Pacific Ocean is in danger. People pollute its waters.

Overfishing, or fishing too much, causes many **marine** animals to become **extinct**.

Words to Know

continents (KAHN-tuh-nuhnts): the large landmasses of Earth, including Asia, Africa, Europe, North America, South America, Australia, and Antarctica

earthquakes (URTH-kwayks): periods of sudden, violent shaking of the ground, caused by movements of Earth's surface, that may damage buildings and cause injuries

endangered (en-DAYN-jurd): threatened; in danger of becoming extinct

equator (i-KWAY-tur): an imaginary line around the middle of Earth that is an equal distance from the North and South Poles

explorer (ik-SPLOR-ur): a person who travels to an unknown area

extinct (ik-STINGKT): no longer existing

marine (muh-REEN): having to do with the ocean

Index

animals 16, 18, 21
continents 3, 4, 5, 11
deep(est) 12, 13, 18
equator 6, 7
Magellan, Ferdinand 8, 9
overfishing 21
sea otters 18, 19
volcanoes 14

Comprehension Questions

1. True or False: The Pacific Ocean is the biggest ocean in the world.
2. True or False: The equator separates the North and South Pacific Oceans.
3. True or False: The Pacific Ocean got its name from Ferdinand Magellan.
4. True or False: The Pacific Ocean is two feet deep.
5. True or False: The Pacific Ocean is in danger due to overfishing.

Answers
1. True 2. True 3. True 4. False 5. True

About the Author

Lauren Gordon is originally from New York and now lives in Florida. She lives with her husband and two children. In her free time, she likes to read and spend time with her family.

Written by: Lauren Gordon
Design by: Jen Bowers
Editor: Kim Thompson

Photographs from Shutterstock.com: Cover and p.15 image ©2020 Leonardo Gonzalez, backgound ©2012 Andrey_Kuzmin, water globe ©2012 zffoto; p.2 and throughout backgroud ©elic; p.3 and throughout background ©Aleksandra Bataeva, globes ©Designua; p.5 ©Pyty; p.7 ©2008 Alex Staroseltsev; p.9 ©Naci Yavuz; p.11 ©2021 Artsiom P; p.13 ©2019 Oliver Denker; p.17 ©2015 Leonardo Gonzalez; p.19 ©2017 rbrown10, ©2018 Imagine Earth Photography; p.20-21 ©2018 David A Litman

Library of Congress PCN Data
Oceans of the World / Gordon
The Pacific Ocean
ISBN 978-1-63897-448-2 (hard cover)
ISBN 978-1-63897-563-2 (paperback)
ISBN 978-1-63897-678-3 (EPUB)
ISBN 978-1-63897-793-3 (eBook)
Library of Congress Control Number: 2021953366

Printed in the United States of America.

Seahorse Publishing Company
www.seahorsepub.com

Published in the United States
Seahorse Publishing
PO Box 771325
Coral Springs, FL 33077

SEAHORSE PUBLISHING